THE LIBRARY OF THE WESTERN HEMISPHERE™

Exploring CHILE

with the FIVE Themes of Geography

by Jane Holiday

The Rosen Publishing Group's
PowerKids Press™
New York

Published in 2005 by The Rosen Publishing Group, Inc.
29 East 21st Street, New York, NY 10010

First Edition

Editor: Geeta Sobha
Book Design: Michelle Innes

Photo Credits: Cover, p. 1 © William J. Hebert/Getty Images; p. 9 © Dave G. Houser/Corbis; p. 9 (glacier) © Craig Lovell/Corbis; p. 10 © Jeremy Horner/Corbis; p. 10 (Atacama Desert) © Hubert Stadler/Corbis; pp. 10 (stone statues), 21 (mountains) © Art Wolfe/Getty Images; p. 12 © Barnabas Bosshart/Corbis; p. 12 (Valparaíso) © Walter Bibikow/Getty Images; p. 15 © Carlos Barria/Reuters/Corbis; pp. 15 (Chuquicamata), 16 (vineyard) © Charles O'Rear/Corbis; p. 16 © Nicholas DeVore/Getty Images; p. 17 © Galen Rowell/Corbis; p. 19 © Paul A. Sounders/Corbis; p. 19 (boats) © Paul Almasy/Corbis; p. 21 (coast) © Chad Ehlers/Getty Images

Library of Congress Cataloging-in-Publication Data

Holiday, Jane.
Exploring Chile with the five themes of geography / by Jane Holiday.— 1st ed.
p. cm. — (The library of the western hemisphere)
Includes index.
ISBN 1-4042-2677-X (lib. bdg.) — ISBN 0-8239-4637-1 (pbk.)
1. Chile—Geography—Juvenile literature. I. Title. II. Series.

F3060.9.H65 2005
918.3—dc22

2004003823

Manufactured in the United States of America

Contents

The FIVE Themes of Geography

Geography is the study of Earth, including its physical features, climate, resources, and people. To study a particular country or area, such as Chile, geographers use the five themes of geography: location, place, human-environment interaction, movement, and regions. These themes help us organize and understand important information about the geography of places around the world. Let's find out about the geography of Chile, using the five themes.

1 Location

Where is Chile?

Chile can be found by using its absolute, or exact, location. Absolute location tells exactly where a place is in the world. The imaginary lines of longitude and latitude are used to find the absolute location of a place.

Chile can also be found by using its relative, or general, location. Relative location tells where a place is in relation to other places, such as countries or bodies of water, that are nearby. Relative location can also be defined by using the cardinal directions of east, west, north, and south.

2 Place

What is Chile like?

By looking at Chile's physical and human features, we can get to know the land and the people. Physical features occur in nature. Bodies of water, landforms, climate, and plant and animal life are all examples of physical features. Human features are things, such as buildings, cities, and governments, that people have created.

3 Human-Environment Interaction

How do the people and the environment of Chile affect each other?

Human-environment interaction shows how the environment of Chile has affected the way the people live. Also, it explains how people in Chile have adapted to, or changed to fit, their environment.

4 Movement

How do people, goods, and ideas get from place to place in Chile?

Movement explains how products, people, and ideas move around the country. It also shows how they move from Chile to other countries in the world.

5 Regions

What does Chile have in common with other places around the world? What features do places within Chile share to make them part of a region?

Places are grouped into regions by physical and cultural features that they share. We will study the features that Chile shares with other areas, making it part of a certain region. We'll also look at physical and political regions within Chile.

1 Location

Chile's absolute location is 30° south and 71° west.

Chile's relative location can be determined by looking at the places that surround it. Chile is bordered by Peru on the north. Bolivia and Argentina border Chile on the east. The Pacific Ocean lies on the west coast of Chile.

Chile is located along the western coast of South America. It is in the southern part of South America.

Where in the World?

Absolute location is the point where the lines of longitude and latitude meet.

Longitude tells a place's position in degrees east or west of the prime meridian, a line that runs through Greenwich, London.

Latitude tells a place's position in degrees north or south of the equator, the imaginary line that goes around the middle of the earth.

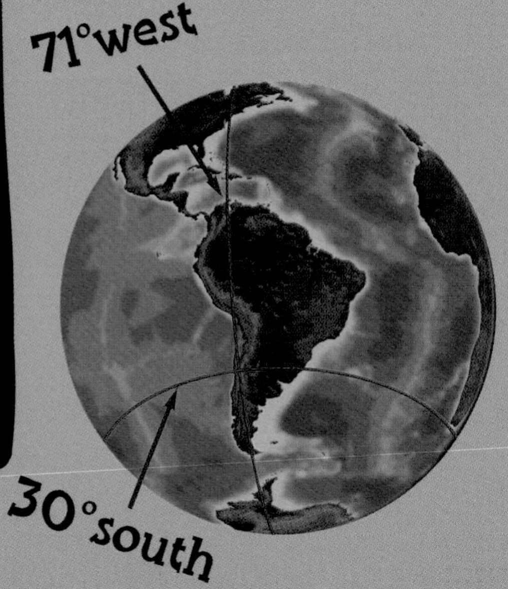

71°west

30°south

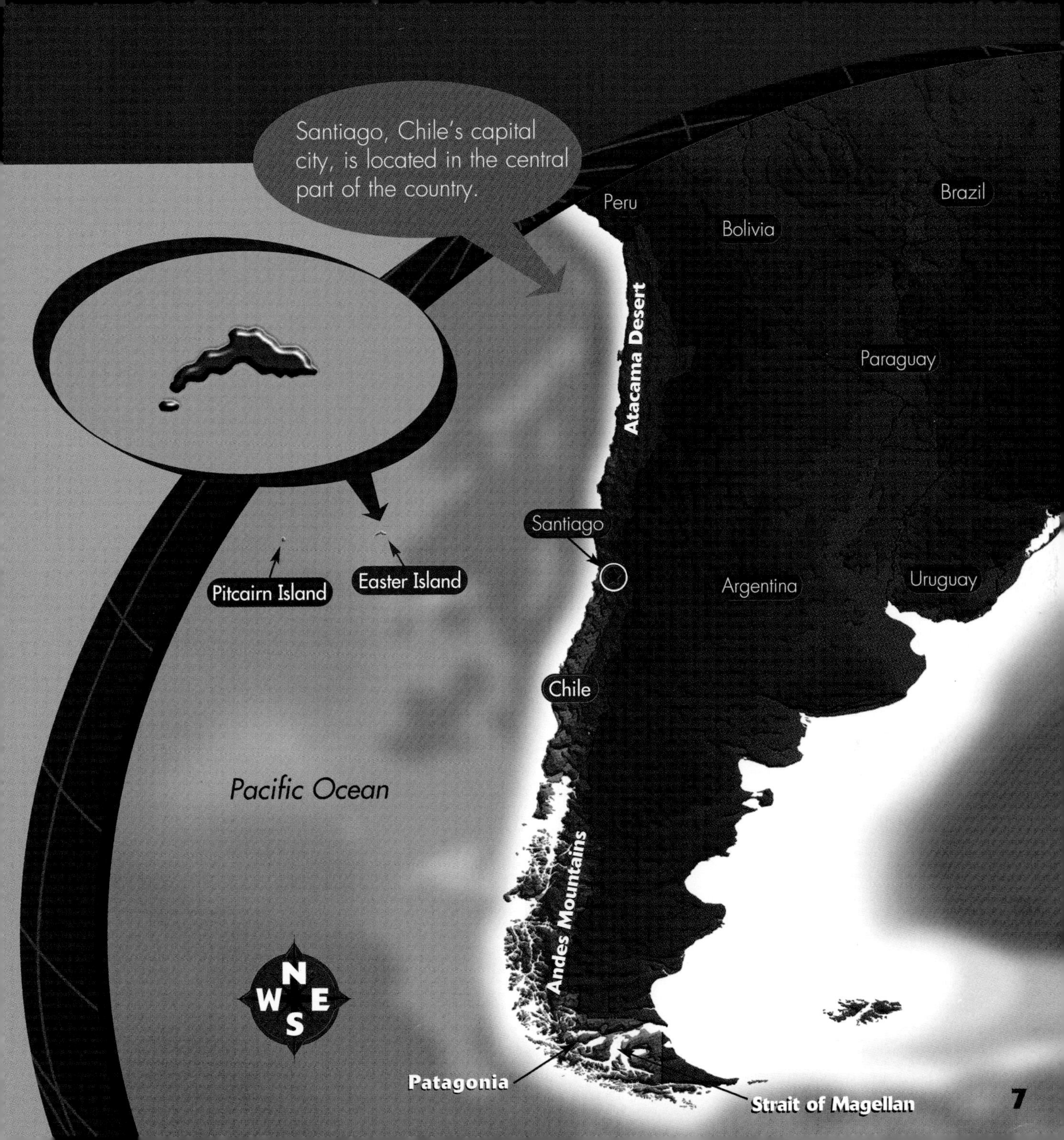
Santiago, Chile's capital city, is located in the central part of the country.
Peru
Brazil
Bolivia
Atacama Desert
Paraguay
Santiago
Pitcairn Island
Easter Island
Argentina
Uruguay
Chile
Pacific Ocean
Andes Mountains
N
W
E
S
Patagonia
Strait of Magellan

2 Place

Physical Features

Chile can be divided into three physical areas: the Chilean Andes, the plateau area, and the coastal mountains. The Chilean Andes are mountains in the east of the country. There are many volcanoes in the Andes. About fifty of them are still active. The mountains are from 16,500 to 19,500 feet (5,029 to 5,944 meters) high. The plateau area includes the Central Valley, which is made up of fertile farmland. The coastal mountains, in the west of Chile, reach about 6,500 feet (1,981 m) in height.

Chile's climate varies by region. The northern region is a desert area that gets very little rain. The Atacama Desert is found here. The central region has a moderate climate, with temperatures between 54° and 85°F (12° and 29°C). The southern region is a cool area

Some of the glaciers found in southern Chile are thought to be a million years old. When pieces of glaciers break off, they become floating icebergs.

The llareta plant grows in the Atacama Desert. This rare plant grows less than half an inch a year.

In parts of the Atacama Desert, there are no records of rain having ever fallen.

Chile owns Easter Island, in the Pacific Ocean about 2,200 miles (3,540 kilometers) west of the mainland. The island is home to gigantic stone statues made about 1,300 years ago.

The Andean condor is Chile's national bird and the largest flying bird.

that gets about 200 inches (508 centimeters) of rain per year. The areas of Tierra del Fuego and Patagonia experience strong snowstorms.

Chile owns the islands along its southern coast. These include the Juan Fernandez Islands and two-thirds of the islands of Tierra del Fuego. Argentina owns the rest of Tierra del Fuego.

There is a variety of plant life in Chile. The tamarugo grows in the desert. The Chilean pine tree and cacti can be found in the Central Valley. In the rain forest of the south, laurel, magnolia, and Chilean cedar grow.

The animals of Chile include pumas, Andean wolves, llamas, vicuñas, flamingoes, and condors. There are also huemuls and pudus, which are types of deer, and the carancho, which is a bird of prey.

Chile's National Congress is located in the city of Valparaíso.

This government building in Santiago was built in 1875. It was once used by Chile's National Congress.

Human Features

Over 15,665,000 people live in Chile. The majority of the people live in the Central Valley area, in and around Chile's four largest cities—Santiago, Valparaíso, Viña del Mar, and Concepción.

Most Chileans are mestizos, people who are descended from both Spanish and Native American peoples. The Araucanians are the native people of Chile. Chile was a colony of Spain from the 1500s to 1810. Spanish is the official language of Chile. Spanish architecture can be seen in the Iglesia de San Francisco, which was built in 1618, and Casa de Manso de Velasco, built in 1730.

Chile's form of government is called a representative democracy. The president is elected by the people, and is only allowed to serve for one six-year term.

3 Human-Environment Interaction

Chile's climate influences how and where people live. The climate of the south is excellent for sheep farming. However, only 3 percent of the population live there due to the cold and rainy weather. The moderate weather in the center of the country has attracted much of the population. In the Atacama Desert in the north, most towns are along the coast.

Chileans rely on the natural resources of their country. Minerals such as copper, silver, iron ore, and gold are mined. Petroleum and natural gas are found in the Strait of Magellan, at the southern tip of Chile. Chile's rivers are used to provide hydroelectric power, an important energy source. Chileans also use the heat of the volcanoes as an energy source. The volcanic ash helps to make fertile soil that is important for farming.

Chile's farmers in the Central Valley grow wheat, corn,

This copper mine in Chuquicamata, in northern Chile, is one of the largest in the world.

Freshwater fish such as salmon are raised for sale to foreign countries.

Grapes for making wine are grown in the Central Valley.

Tourists travel to Chile to view its active volcanoes, such as this one in Villarrica.

beans, rice, and potatoes. Fruits, such as grapes and apples, are grown for sale to other countries. Fishermen catch sardines, mackerel, and anchovies.

Chile's environmental problems are a result of human activity. The factories and cars in Santiago are the main causes of air pollution. Santiago is located in a valley with high mountains on either side, so air does not flow in and out easily. This causes polluted air to stay in the atmosphere over the city. Mining has resulted in air pollution as well as water pollution. The forests of Chile are being reduced as trees are cut down for timber. Chile's government is working to protect the environment with laws.

Sheep farming takes place in the south of Chile.

4 Movement

Chileans depend on a variety of transportation to get around their country. The Pan-American Highway, which connects South America and North America, goes through Chile. Cities along Chile's coast use ocean routes to move goods. Airplanes are used to reach places, such as Coihayque, that are difficult to get to.

Ports such as Valparaíso and San Antonio are used to export goods. The Strait of Magellan is a shipping lane between the Atlantic and Pacific Oceans. Arturo Merino Benítez Airport allows travel in and out of Chile. Railroads connect Chile to Peru, Boliva, and Argentina.

Chile has over 60 television stations and over 200 radio stations. Newspapers include *El Mercurio*, *La Nación*, and *La Tercera de la Hora*. Many of Chile's writers have gained international recognition. Pablo Neruda and Gabriela Mistral have won the Nobel Prize for Literature.

Quintay is a fishing village on the Pacific coast, south of Valparaíso.

There are 49,594 miles (79,814 km) of highway in Chile. However, only 9,621 miles (15,484 km) are paved.

5 Regions

Chile is part of cultural and geographic regions. Chile is part of the cultural region known as Latin America, where most people speak a Romance language, such as Spanish, French, or Portuguese. Latin America is made up of countries in the Western Hemisphere south of the United States, including the West Indies.

Chile is within the geographical region called the Ring of Fire. This is an area that goes around the Pacific Ocean. Many earthquakes and volcanoes occur in this region.

Within Chile, there are land regions—the Andes, the plateau area, and the coastal mountains. There are also weather regions: the dry north, the mild central region, and the cold south. Chile is also divided into 13 political sections called regions.

Chile's 13 regions are broken down into provinces and municipalities.

Tarapacá
Antofagasta
Atacama
Coquimbo
Santiago
Valparaíso
Maule
O'Higgins
Bio-Bío
Araucanía
Los Lagos
Aisén
Magallanés y de la Antarctica

Bahia Inglesia is an area in the Atacama region where many people vacation.

Torres del Paine National Park is located in the Magallanés y de la Antarctica region.

FACT ZONE

Chile's Flag

Population (2003) 15,665,216

Language Spanish

Absolute location 30° south, 71° west

Capital city Santiago

Area 292,135 square miles (756,626 square kilometers)

Highest point Nevado Ojos del Salado 22,600 feet (6,888 meters)

Lowest point Pacific Ocean zero feet

Land boundaries Argentina, Bolivia, and Peru

Natural resources copper, timber, iron ore, nitrates, precious metals, and molybdenum

Agricultural products grapes, apples, wheat, sugar beets, tomatoes, potatoes, maize, wood and wood products, and livestock

Major exports copper, fishmeal, fruits, vegetables, paper and paper products, and chemical products

Major imports machinery, transportation equipment, and chemical and mineral products

Glossary

culture (KUHL-chur) The way of life, ideas, customs, and traditions shared by a group of people.

democracy (di-MOK-ruh-see) A way of governing a country in which the people choose their leaders in elections.

fertile (FUR-tuhl) Able to grow plenty of plants.

hydroelectric power (hye-droh-i-LEK-trik POU-ur) Water power that is used to turn a generator to produce electricity.

interaction (in-tur-AK-shuhn) The action between people, groups, or things.

plateau (pla-TOH) An area of high, flat land.

province (PROV-uhnss) A district or a region of some countries.

region (REE-juhn) An area or a district.

resource (ri-SORSS) Something that is valuable or useful to a place or person.

volcano (vol-KA-noh) A mountain with an opening through which steam, ashes, and lava are sometimes forced out.

Index

Web Sites

Due to the changing nature of Internet links, PowerKids Press has developed an on-line list of Web sites related to the subject of this book. This site is updated regularly. Please use this link to access the list:
http://www.powerkidslinks.com/lwh/chile